The Barnyard Bandit

by LaToya Simms
illustrated by John Wallner

 HOUGHTON MIFFLIN HARCOURT
School Publishers

Copyright © by Houghton Mifflin Harcourt Publishing Company

Printed in China

ISBN-13: 978-0-547-02733-3
ISBN-10: 0-547-02733-8

3 4 5 6 7 8 0940 18 17 16 15 14 13 12 11 10

Spinner the spider was
hungry. She hurried to her web
to see if she had trapped any
bugs for breakfast. That was
when she saw that her web was
missing.

"A bandit has been here!"
Spinner cried.

2

Hank the horse poked his head over his stall door. "What happened?"

"My web is gone."

"Maybe you just forgot where you made it," said Fuzz the cat.

Spinner looked hurt. "I
worked hard to weave that web.
Now I have no food, and it will
take all day to make a new web."

Just then, Hank let out a
snort. "My hay!" he cried.

"Someone took my special hay!" he said. "Each day, I collect the sweetest bits of hay from my meal. I save them for a treat."

"We need to catch the bandit who is taking our special things," said Spinner.

Just then, Fuzz let out a loud "Meow!" He held up a tiny ball of red yarn. "I had a big ball of yarn and NOW look at it! Someone has been stealing it."

Fuzz looked at Hank and Spinner. "Don't just stand there. Go catch that yarn bandit!"

"I have an idea," said
Spinner. "I'll make a new web.
When the bandit tries to take it,
we'll catch him."

Spinner's new web was almost
six feet wide! Hank, Fuzz, and
Spinner hid behind a pile of hay
and waited.

The three friends grew tired
and fell asleep. They woke up
and saw that the web was gone!
The bandit had struck again!

Spinner studied the ground.
"There aren't any footprints,"
she said. "But I see something."

Spinner came closer. "I see
feathers," she said. "Now I
know why we didn't find
footprints. Our bandit can fly!"

The clues led to a big bush.
Hank, Spinner, and Fuzz peeked
through the leaves of the bush.

9

"Hello," said a bird. She was sitting on a nest made out of the yarn, hay, and web. Eggs sat in the nest.

The three friends smiled. The bird needed their special things more than they did.

Responding

Cause and Effect

What does the barnyard bandit
do in this story? Why does she
do it? Make a chart.

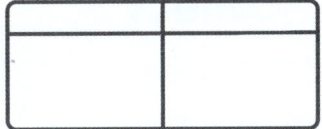

✏ Talk About It

Text to Text Think of another
story about someone who loses
something. How does he or she
feel? How does he or she find
what was lost?

WORDS TO KNOW

almost	gone	idea
any	happened	leaves
behind	hello	

LEARN MORE WORDS

| bandit | collect | weave |

TARGET SKILL **Cause and Effect**
Tell what happens and why.

TARGET STRATEGY **Visualize** Picture
what is happening as you read.

GENRE A **mystery** is a story about
a character who solves a puzzle.